Yet I Will Joy

Yet I Will Joy

Poems of Faith and Hope

by
Valerie P. Graham

RESOURCE *Publications* • Eugene, Oregon

YET I WILL JOY
Poems of Faith and Hope

Copyright © 2019 Valerie P. Graham. All rights reserved. Except for brief quotations in critical publications or reviews, no part of this book may be reproduced in any manner without prior written permission from the publisher. Write: Permissions, Wipf and Stock Publishers, 199 W. 8th Ave., Suite 3, Eugene, OR 97401.

Resource Publications
An Imprint of Wipf and Stock Publishers
199 W. 8th Ave., Suite 3
Eugene, OR 97401

www.wipfandstock.com

PAPERBACK ISBN: 978-1-5326-8127-1
HARDCOVER ISBN: 978-1-5326-8128-8
EBOOK ISBN: 978-1-5326-8129-5

Manufactured in the U.S.A.   08/05/19

To the glory of the blessed Trinity—
God the Father, God the Son, and God the Holy Spirit—
Always faithful in his works and ways.

Contents

Preface | ix

The Idol | 1
The Foe | 2
Sweet Joy | 4
Enduring Hope | 6
My Lord, Ruler of My Life | 7
"What Would You Have Me Do for You?" | 10
In Covenant | 14
The Calm and the Storm | 16
Exult in God, the God of Hope | 18
Though All This, Yet I Will Joy | 19
Washed Clean | 22
Reminded to Rejoice | 23
Another Comforter to Send | 24
The Breath of Life | 25
The Lord Calls | 27
To Live for You Alone | 29
By Its Fruit | 30
Love, Peace, Joy | 31
The Test | 32
The Calling of the Princess | 34

Preface

"Yet I Will Joy: Poems of Faith and Hope" is the product of thirty years' writing and reflections. During these years I trained in the inductive methods of Bible study through Precept Ministries, Inc. After participating in various group studies using the Precept Upon Precept® studies, I began to lead these studies and continued to do so for over 20 years. Through hours of meditation and study, my heart would sing the hope, the promises, and the truth of God's word. These songs that flowed from my heart are reflected in this collection of poems.

With a cancer diagnosis in 2011, faith and hope were anchored deeper within my heart, and they became more prominent in these writings. Faith and hope in Jesus Christ, the Son of the living God, had truly become the reason and joy of the life I was living.

At this point, I began to transition more from teaching Bible studies to Biblical lay counseling. It is my firm conviction that the Bible with its truth and principles gives us everything we need to live godly in this life (2 Peter 1:3). So in the journey through the poems, there is a focus on the heart—and the choices that are made from the heart—which is at the core of Biblical change.

The last poem "The Calling of the Princess" is a fairytale story poem that pictures the outcast slave as a princess whom the Prince would redeem. Once she is redeemed, he would make her his bride. This is a picture of every believer whose faith and hope is anchored in Jesus Christ.

It is true in our Christian journey of faith and hope that we do not do it alone. There are many that come along beside us to teach, train, and encourage us. This has also been true in the journey to publish this book.

I am most indebted to my beloved husband, who has not only been with me every step of the way, but would light a fire under me when I began to lag behind and doubt. Thank you, my dearly beloved husband. I am also thankful for the encouragement of family and friends.

To Kallie Falandays and Tell Tell Poetry, thank you for patiently walking beside me through the editing process. Your diligence helped bring these poems into a cohesive collection.

With heartfelt gratitude, thank you Wipf and Stock for publishing this book. I am most grateful for the services you rendered to publish this book that it may be of service for the Lord to his glory.

Thank you to all those who lifted prayers to our heavenly Father that this book might be used to his honor and glory. My desire is that these poems will capture the heart and imagination of the reader so that their faith is deepened and their hope is strengthened to the praise, honor and glory of the Lord Jesus Christ.

The Idol

The idol sits there on the table made of solid stone.
Its ears are carved so gracefully with smooth and gentle curves;
Yet as words are spoken, these ears hear not a sound.
Its eyes are tediously molded, each lash and brow detailed;
Yet scenes of beauty that surround are but as darkest night.
Its nose is shaped and chiseled, proportions made exact;
Yet sweet perfume of roses, it shall never smell.
Its lips are formed with tenderness as if a word it would speak;
Yet words are never spoken to break the dreadful silence.

The idol sits there on the table; its worth is up for bid.
It brings a bid from artists; they rave *magnificent*.
It brings a bid from merchants; they plot their gain of wealth.
It brings a bid from craftsmen; they marvel at its workmanship.

The idol sits within my heart made by me myself.
I carved the ears precisely to frequencies of merriment;
Yet 'midst the droning noisiness, God's whispers it fails to hear.
I molded eyes to catch the sparkles of gold and diamond gems;
Yet nature's beauty all around, God's glory clouded is.
I shaped the nose so nature's scents it would whiff;
Yet the fragrance of God's Son, the Rose of Sharon, not a sniff.
I formed its lips to boast my pride, achievements and awards;
Yet in the din of accolades, God's praises it does not sing.

The idol sits within my heart; its worth is up for bid.
It brings a bid from loved ones: broken hearts, heated tears, deserted love.
It brings a bid from God Almighty: eternal death its price.
It brings a bid from me myself; its worth I must decide.

The Foe

The foe, the foe, the deadly foe,
His presence seek to know.
He lurks at noon and night and day
To kill those whom he may.

To take your soul to death with him
Is his eternal whim.
To save your soul, and not be lost,
My friend, just count the cost.

What is the cost of life so dear?
The answer is so near.
It is the cost of death to self
That brings your soul's good health.

For death of self with no remain
Will turn your loss to gain.
In Christ alone, yes, through his blood
There comes the cleansing flood.

Do you the cost consider high
That to yourself must die?
Christ paid the price; he gave his all;
Why does this so appall?

If in Christ's love, he's made you friend
Ought you not seek to spend
Your days his goodness to impart,
His cross to take to heart?

Now open wide your eyes; take heed
If 'gainst the foe you speed;
The greatest lie that he does stoke:
"The cross is but a joke."

The foe's grand scheme to play the game:
Appetite for a name,
The fight for rights, entitlement,
The quarreling, strife, embattlements.

For those enlisted in his ploy
Are now all pawns, a toy.
The end is sure and certain fire
For those caught in this mire.

Oh! Fight the foe, yes, fight the foe
That causes so much woe.
Oh! Fight with life, the living Word,
And sing till all have heard:

The foe has lost, the foe has lost;
In the cross is our boast.
For Christ has won upon that tree
Our final victory.

Now closely note and take your stand:
Are you a foe or friend?
The foe receives his justice due,
But we with Christ his praise pursue.

Sweet Joy

Sweet joy comes in the morning new
With song afloat, aloft in heart:
      Mercies sweet, mercies new,
      Mercies fresh, mercies true.
Grief does leave, yes, to depart.

That night so dark, no water 'round,
For living streams my soul did thirst:
      Waters sweet; waters pure;
      Waters still, sure to cure;
Waters from the Rock that bursts.

Though dark the night, the morning comes;
Its line goes out through all the earth:
      Dark to light, dark now bright,
      Black to white, all now sight.
Dawn brings forth a soul of mirth.

So early does my soul seek Thee.
It longs for Thee, to see Thy power:
      Power to help, power to heal,
      Power to rule, power to fill
Thirsting souls with rains that shower.

The morning breaks; sweet joy is come!
The weeping, ah, was but a night:
      Dark and drear, cold with fear,
      Blackest gloom, panic near;
All's dispelled in brightest light.

From blackest darkness of my sin
He welcomed me into the light,
    Rescued me by his grace,
    Purchased me, set my face
Seeing him in his great might.

Sweet joy comes with the rising Son,
His rays beam out with light divine:
    Light to warm, comfort still,
    Light of life, joy to feel.
In the Savior, joy is mine!

Enduring Hope

Dreams are thoughts within my mind
    Of things that might now be.
But hope is written in God's Word
    Of what shall surely be.

Dreams are fleeting thoughts of pleasure
    Rooted in this world.
But hope is stayed on God himself:
    The one who died for me.

Dreams are sketched with ink by men
    To plan for happiness.
But hope is etched with God's own blood
    Securing naught but holiness.

Dreams dissolve 'midst toil and stress,
    Yes, suff'ring, pain, and loneliness.
But hope with faith and love remains
    'Midst trials and tribulations.

Dreams may come and dreams may go
    As circumstances alter.
But hope grows strong to God's great glory
    Waiting for the promise.

Dreams may boast the work of man:
    His strength, his pride, and glory.
But hope exults in God above
    To glorify his Name.

So why do I spend so much thought
    On that which lasts a moment?
When hope endures eternity,
    An anchor for my soul.

My Lord, Ruler of My Life

In early days my eyes were blind,
No light outside myself.
I lived in pride and selfishness,
No kindness others showed.

I went along my merry way,
My life in my control.
I grumbled, murmured, and complained,
No good in others saw.

Who was that God that bid me live
With others kept in mind?
I thought God owed me happiness,
No pain, but ease and play.

I am the center of my world,
God's law I need not heed:
To choose to disobey is sin
Your life to death will lose.

Just how could God so boldly think
That he would rule my life?
I am my own; I choose my path;
I'll walk the way I choose.

My eyes were blind and saw no light;
I pushed aside God's truth.
So I'm without excuse or hope—
A guilty sinner charged.

I looked for help, an advocate,
To intercede for me.
Jesus, the Son of God, stepped forth
To plead in my defense.

He stood before the Judge of all,
He pled his blood for me.
That blood poured out for all my sin
While on the cross he hung.

The Judge declared me free from sin—
A gracious, precious gift—
Secured by Jesus Christ, my Lord;
By faith I do receive.

Now justified by faith alone,
I have his peace, his love.
I sing the praise of God above;
Through Christ I'm reconciled.

This peace I've never known before
Has settled in my soul;
It can endure through stormy times,
A refuge, free from fear.

This love, that he would give his life,
Though I forsook his word,
To give me life and hope again,
Is grace beyond compare.

Redeemed from sin! Redeemed from sin!
I died with him that day.
He took my sin and gave me life;
I live for him today.

My heart does yearn his will to do;
It is my pure delight.
I choose to die to selfish ways
To live to please my Lord.

I now no condemnation know,
For I'm in Jesus Christ.
I am set free from sin and death;
His Spirit is the proof.

My mind is set on truth divine,
Walking in his Spirit.
And by his Spirit I am led
To bear forth fruit for God.

The fruit of holiness displays
As pause before I speak
To think how I might honor Christ
And show I live for him.

Who is this God that bids me live
With others kept in mind?
My Lord, the ruler of my life;
All glory is to him!

"What Would You Have Me Do for You?"

Mark 10:46–52

The beggar, blind, sat by the way
As many days before
In hopes that coins, say one or two,
Be cast to him that day.

A noise, a throng, a crowd came near;
"Who was this passing by?"
"Jesus of Nazareth," he heard
In whispered wonderment.

That name of Jesus pierced his mind;
A cry welled up within,
"O Jesus, thou Son of David,
Have mercy upon me!"

He did not know if Jesus heard,
Or if response would make.
He only knew the one of God
Alone could mercy give.

Voices warned, rebuked, "Be quiet,
To him no word do speak."
Yet all the more his cries went out,
To Jesus made his plea.

His cries were heard and favor gained;
The Son of God did say,
"Call him before me to appear."
He heard, "Take heart, come near."

"My child, I've heard your mercy plea;
What would you have me do?"
The beggar blind replied straightway,
"Let me my sight receive."

As simply as he called him, "Come,"
He bid him, "Go your way;
Your faith has made the darkness light;
Your sight is now made bright."

The beggar blind rejoiced, now whole,
With sight, fresh faith, new life.
His joy abounded with delight,
He turned and followed Christ.

The beggar asked for sight to see:
Night to flee, light to shine,
A heart aglow with holiness
To lead him in God's peace.

Then with Jesus he walked in light
In fellowship and joy,
His heart transformed by mercy's plea,
His sinner's soul set free.

I'm sitting here a beggar blind,
A noise of crowd peels forth.
I strain to know, "Who's passing by?"
Jesus, the Son of God!

His gift of mercy is well known.
Will I his mercy seek?
What heart's desire yearns in my soul
That I can't satisfy?

Is there a gift he might bestow
To give a lasting hope
For sorrow, pain, and loneliness:
The burdens of my soul?

Is there a favor, kindness bold,
To cleanse my soul of sin,
To rid my conscience of its pangs
Of grief, of shame, of guilt?

O yes, his mercy I will seek;
I am a beggar blind.
I have no sight to see through pain,
Through clouds of suffering.

I have no hope that life is more
Than drudgery and toil,
And all that is my happiness
Is but a fleeting thought.

The crowd is streaming like a wave,
Its billows to o'erwhelm.
Jesus, the Son of God strides close,
I cry, I weep aloud,

"Jesus, the Son of God, my Lord,
Have mercy upon me!"
He speaks, "My child, your plea I hear.
What would you have me do?"

My words pour forth this mercy plea,
"Forgive me of my sins;
Create in me a heart that's clean,
So I may live with you."

The Lord moves closer, and he stops
To touch my blinded eyes,
To prove to me that he alone
Does meet my soul's desire.

I run into his arms with joy
To him to ever cling.
I'll never fear to ask of him
New mercies for my soul.

In Covenant

The radiance of your glory
Shone as you stood with me
And bid me *Come* in cov'nant,
Then sealed me in your blood.

My guilt and shame I gave you
With my pain and sorrow,
My transgressions without end:
A robe like filthy soot.

Deadly sin the robe I gave,
Your death would pay its cost.
There in flesh and blood to save,
You wore it on the cross.

Your soul travailed to vict'ry,
From death your body rose
Transcending into glory:
The Son of God's new clothes.

You're clothed in power and justice,
In strength of majesty.
You wear love, mercy, kindness
And wrap me in these robes.

You in your cov'nant sealed me,
In me poured life anew,
Then clothed in robes so lovely
That glow a brilliant hue.

I stumbled being helpless;
Your cov'nant strength I sought.
Your Spirit breathed with freshness,
New strength within was wrought.

The enemy before me
Falls to your mighty sword.
He stands not in your glory,
Your power, might, as Lord.

No foe can overtake me,
For you are pledged to be
My Savior in the Cov'nant
For all eternity.

The Calm and the Storm

The quiet calm spreads o'er the land;
I sense its still repose.
It bids me work and toil the ground;
The storm approaches fast.

The storm moves in, the lightnings strike,
the thunders mighty roar.
The heavens cast the blackest night;
the rains like rivers pour.

*O Lord, I cry, the seeds beneath
Have yet a leaf or bud;
Oh, let them grow to fruitful flow'r,
Not lost in waters deep.*

*These seeds the gifts from hands of heav'n
In tenderness were sown,
Then nourished in your loving grace
Your glory to display.*

*Oh, save your seeds and shelter them,
for in your name they grow.
And in your name they'll beauty show
Until the harvest comes.*

The Lord stretched forth his quick'ning hand,
And sheltered them from harm,
From all that sought to kill, destroy,
Uproot his precious seed.

He swiftly caught each lightning bolt.
He hushed the thunder's roar.
He blew the clouds of rain away
And caused the sun to shine.

The storm has passed; the light shines forth
On wonders of his work.
The precious work is seen in growth
Of seed thus safely kept.

The calm before was to take heed
The seeds be rooted deep,
So through the storm they'd anchored be
To thrive and praise the Lord.

My soul is planted in God's word;
The Lord's my guardian.
Through the calm my hope's established;
The storm shows true my faith.

Oh, praise him in the calm repose
With hands that work his truth,
So that the soul be fit to meet
The storm just o'er the hill.

Exult in God, the God of Hope

Exult in God, the God of hope;
Great hope he gives to me.
This hope rests in his promises
Of mercy, grace, and peace.

Lord, of your mercies I will sing:
All my sins you forgive;
My iniquities you blot out;
My heart's restored to you.

Your grace, a gift to revel in,
Abundant and divine,
Transcends my heart from worldliness
To heights of majesty.

In peace I now know fellowship
With Father and the Son;
Because your Spirit lives in me
There's blessed harmony.

My hope rests in God's promises
Of mercy, grace, and peace.
Oh, yes! I will exult in God;
The God of hope: my hope!

Though All This, Yet I Will Joy

Habakkuk 3:16-19

The call came in, results were told.
I heard the news, the dread confirmed.
My body trembled;
My lips quivered at the voice;
My mind reeled at what was to come:
Pain, sickness, surgery, chemo.

And though I trembled in myself,
I prayed that I might have peace in my soul,
Rest in him in the day of trouble.
Yes, my body would be assaulted;
The tumor enlarged would invade,
Invade with all its powers to destroy.

Yet I will have peace through the terrible days.
Yet I will rejoice in the Lord my God.

I will rejoice in the Lord my God:
Though the tumor invade the tissue of the breast,
     Growing in size and feeding on health;
Though medicines flow into the veins that fight the foe,
     The battle brings nausea, pain and discomfort,
     Strength is exhausted, the mind cannot focus;
Though the long golden hair, the glory once given,
     Is now required a gift to the Lord;
Though the body writhes in anguish
     and despair assails the mind;
Though the war rages on within the body,
     And the knife is wielded to cut it asunder,
     Carving out the viscous attacker,
     Leaving scars and tedious recovery;

Though the rays of the sun many times stronger
> Must pierce through the body,
> Leaving their marks and tender redness;
Though all this come upon me,
Yet I will rejoice in the Lord my God.

I will joy in the Lord God of my salvation:
> *For he chose me before the foundation of the world,*
>> *Before having done either good or bad;*
> *For he demonstrated his love to me while I was still his enemy;*
> *For he demonstrated his love toward me in his son's death;*
> *For he paid the debt of death I owed for sin but could not pay;*
> *For he redeemed me from sin, death, and the grave;*
> *For he redeemed me to serve a living God;*
> *For he forgave me all my sins in the blood of Christ, his son;*
> *For he secured salvation for me with his indwelling Spirit*
>> *And grows within me daily his lovely fruit—*
>>> *love, joy, peace, patience, kindness, goodness,*
>>> *faithfulness, gentleness, and self-control;*
> *For he has given me everything needful for life and godliness;*
> *For he fitted me in his armor to stand firm as his soldier with*
>> *The belt of truth,*
>> *The breastplate of righteousness,*
>> *The shoes of the gospel of peace,*
>> *The shield of faith,*
>> *The helmet of salvation, and*
>> *The sword of the Spirit, the word of God;*
> *For he trains my hands and fingers for war;*
> *For he is ever with me; he never leaves me or forsakes me;*
> *For he has given me access to himself in his Spirit;*
> *For he has given me an intercessor before him in his son;*
> *For he will complete the work of salvation that he has begun in me;*
> *For he is preparing my eternal home in his presence forever.*
Yes, I will joy in the Lord God of my salvation.

For my salvation is all of him, not of works or anything I have done.
And this very joy itself is a fruit of his Spirit, a gift of himself to me.

Ah, yes! Though the day of trouble comes . . .
Yet I will joy in the Lord God of my salvation,
And he will cause me to walk in his holy ways,
Prepared beforehand that I should walk therein.
Yes, I will joy in the God of my salvation;
There is no greater joy!

Washed Clean

John 13:10

"Not all of you are clean," he said,
Then leaned back in his chair.
Could he be speaking straight to me
Of sin hid deep within?

Oh, let me now search deep inside
To see a spot or blot
That missed the washing white as snow
And still is stained with sin.

He called me follow in his steps
To put aside myself,
Not to rule, in pride o'er others
But humbly serve their needs.

Was that a boast of haughty pride
When I took claim of fame
For all the work that team performed,
To bask in all the glory?

Oh, wash me, Lord, and make me clean
That I may be like you.
You served; you loved; you died for me
To show me how to live.

With all my heart I seek to serve,
To love, to die for you.
So let me hear those gracious words,
"Now you, my child, are clean."

Reminded to Rejoice

Lord, in this day I find myself
Weighed down with anxiousness.
My mind's distracted and distressed,
A swirling maze of thoughts.
Your word directs the path to take:
Remember who you are.

Remind me, Lord, of truths I've known,
Your Word within me burning:
Rejoice in you my hope and stay.
Rejoice forevermore.
Rejoice, you've come into my heart
To still the raging waves.

Oh! Let my songs of praise ascend
To you my Lord and God,
To you, O God, my peace and calm,
Amidst the raging thoughts.
So I'll this day know who you are
And praise you even more.

Another Comforter to Send

John 14:16

And Jesus prayed the Father
Another Comforter to send:
A Comforter as holy
      as the Son of God above.

This Comforter from God,
The Spirit of his Christ,
A presence in my soul
      as a friend will walk with me.

A Comforter as truthful
      as the way, the truth, the life;
A Comforter of righteousness
      that yields his fruit of peace;
A Comforter beside me
      in trials to strengthen faith;
A Comforter so with me,
      a help in time of need;
A Comforter for living
      the life he has for me;
A Comforter who comforts
      that I may comfort too.

This Comforter is given
To me by grace alone,
To me a filthy sinner,
      a gift of love divine.

And Jesus prayed the Father
Another Comforter to send
That I might be made holy
      as the Son of God above.

The Breath of Life

In the beginning, God created
The heavens, the earth, and man.
Into that man he breathed his life—
A living soul, no death.

And then God gave a simple law,
"Thou shalt not eat thereof."
And with this law, God gave to man
The choice to do his will.

Man chose his pride and broke God's law;
His guilt required his death.
Condemned he stood before his God—
His soul to life was lost.

The spark of life's now cold in death,
No way to pay the debt;
The body's death would soon succumb,
To dust, not God, return.

Then God stepped forth to show his love
Through Jesus Christ his son.
God offered Christ, the sacrifice,
To pay the debt for pride.

Uncondemned I now may stand
And be at peace with Him.
His Spirit gave my soul new life,
So I might walk with God.

This Spirit is God's present help
To live the righteous life,
To walk by faith and not by sight,
To love as I am loved.

This Spirit is my guarantee
Of hope that yet awaits,
That hope that I with him will be
In beauty glorified.

My soul awaits that promised day
He comes to take me home,
And there throughout eternity,
I'll live—a living soul.

The Spirit is that breath of life
That makes my soul anew—
That makes my soul a living soul—
A soul that will not die.

The Lord Calls

Lord, Abraham your servant stirred
From foreign land when you he heard:
Leave your idols and forth go
Pick up the path that I will show.

Go to a land you do not know,
And there great blessing I'll bestow.
Leave behind your old life bare;
Pick up my word and hold with care.

You'll journey through the mountains steep,
The desert land, and waters deep.
Leave your burdens and their snares;
Pick up by faith the heav'nly cares.

Lord, unto me has come your call
To walk before you, leave my all.
Leave the cares that weigh me down;
Pick up the truth that I have found.

Go to a land that you will show,
A land in which you will I know.
Leave behind the fears that kill;
Pick up your peace, your perfect will.

I'll journey through the desert lands
Well-guided only by your hands.
Leave behind that ego, I;
Pick up your Spirit from on high.

I'll journey through the mountains steep.
I'll bend my knee for us to meet.
Leave behind this world in thought;
Pick up the life that you have bought.

I'll journey through the waters deep
Upheld by you, for you do keep.
Leave behind my selfish pride;
Pick up your joy and ride the tide.

Lord, unto me has come your call
To walk before you, leave my all.
Leave behind this land of death;
Pick up your cross, go forth by faith.

To Live for You Alone

The soldiers circled you about,
My Lord, my God, my King.
They stripped you bare, unclothed you stand
That I your robe might wear.

They spit upon your royalty
With foulest stench of breath;
All that my thirst be quenched in you,
The Fountainhead of Life.

Then off they led you to the cross
To crucify you there.
In pain and sorrow, suffering
You stayed upon that tree.

You stayed to give your life for me;
My heart doth bow in awe.
My upraised eyes your face behold:
God's gift of life for me.

What grace, what mercy you have shown!
My heart lifts loud its praise.
With rapture and delight I sing,
Here Lord, I give my all.

I give you all my breath, each word;
My feet unerring walk;
Each thought a captive, take for you
To please you with my mind.

You are my Lord, my God, my king,
My refuge and my strength.
With you, my love, I'm crucified
To live for you alone!

By Its Fruit

Matthew 12:33

By its fruit, a tree is known;
The world the fruit is shown.
That fruit, its kind, the same remains
Until no sap flows through its veins.

I'm like a tree displaying fruit
That's nourished through the root.
The fruit displayed will tell the toll
Of what dwells in my soul.

The Spirit if my soul not bless,
The fruit is of the flesh:
Strife, sorcery, and anger's fire.
Judged by God, "Know my ire."

If in my heart, the Spirit lives,
This fruit within me fills:
Patience, kindness, love, and meekness
And all such loveliness.

By its fruit, my life is known;
My attitudes are sown:
If fleshy deeds, his wrath to face,
Spirit's way, all God's grace!

Love, Peace, Joy

Love came down at Christmas,
All glorious and divine.
This love seeks unity,
In Spirit binds as one.
  In fellowship so sweet,
  The Savior do we meet.

Peace dwells within our hearts;
God's made his peace with us.
In canceling our debts,
We're freed from guilt and shame.
  Communion with our Lord so dear
  Binds close the hearts of us so near.

Joy rang out through the skies
Unbounded and so real.
Our souls sing of his power
To heal our sin-sickness.
  In union with our God and Christ,
  Man's loneliness is past.

The love of God we claim,
Peace beyond compare;
Joy's vict'ries we exalt,
Yes, ceaseless praises sing.
  In Jesus Christ, God's firstborn son,
  We're giv'n the love, peace, joy he's won.

The Test

God sends to me a test this day
To see if I will choose
To demonstrate my love for him
And not my selfish pride.

It is a test through deeds to prove
My heart delights in God;
And others highest good I'll seek
E'en to my own distaste.

This test may simply be to give
A ride to one in need.
My time may be in overdrive;
The sacrifice I'll make.

The test has more to do with heart,
My motive, that's the key.
The heart's response will tell the tale
Through thoughts lived out in deeds.

Did I resent that one who asked
This mercy plea of me?
Did I begrudging give that ride
To not be thought as mean?
Did I think it to be given
For favor in return?

Did I respond in cheerfulness
Delighting in my soul?
Did I respond in gentleness
To soothe their anxiousness?
Did I see this act of kindness
As serving for God's hands?

In this test this day, my Lord,
May I bring you delight
To prove to you and to myself
My faith—through deeds of love.

The Calling of the Princess

I. The Kingdom

In hearts and minds and dreams there dwells
As well in realms unknown
The Kingdom of the Great High King
Most glorious to behold.

The grandeur of its palaces
Are hard expressed in words.
They rise amidst the lofty peaks
Unto the highest heights.

The snow upon the mountain steeps
Is cleanest, purest white.
It glistens in the glowing sun
And melts to flowing streams.

The waters down to valleys flow
And form still quiet pools.
Within the verdant pastures play
Birds and little critters.

The sheep and cattle grazing there
Serenely mill about.
No fear, no harm is present there,
Not even darkest night.

The shepherds and the caretakers
Perform their tasks with ease,
For thorns and thistles all are gone,
No tares or weeds there grow.

The valleys and the mountainsides
Grow plumpest, sweetest fruit:
The best of grass and grain and herbs,
All foods of rarest kind.

II. The Feast

The table of its feasting hall
With finest fare is laid;
Sweet-smelling spices and the wines
Delight with ecstasy.

The servants each and every one
Perform their tasks with joy,
And then are beckoned one and all:
"Come, sit, and join the feast."

The joy within that banquet hall
Ascends in holiness.
The Great High King now bids them hear
His proclamation bold.

"Behold, my son, the true Great Prince.
My very strength is he.
He is my heir, the future king;
He'll reign in righteousness."

Each eye beholds his splendor bright,
His father's likeness sees;
His presence fills the bustling hall,
The glory, his alone.

He strides across the room with ease,
His armor gleaming bright,
His poise commands authority,
Bespeaks nobility.

The king himself now risen turns;
The servants bend the knee.
The Great High Prince his father joins
To sit at his right hand.

III. The Prince's Victory

The Great High Prince has now returned,
From Land Forgotten's realm
Where there in slav'ry dwelled dear ones
From his kingdom stolen.

They worked the garden of the king,
In Land Remembered lived.
Satan, the enemy, attacked
By guile and trickery.

In Land Forgotten there they dwelled
In chains and bound in fear,
Not knowing that their true birthright
In Land Remembered is.

The Prince's task was seek and find
Those souls lost in this plight,
Then pay the price to free their souls
To live with him again.

The ransom price was set so high
None could pay or hope.
So on in toil and misery
They lived forgotten there.

The Great High Prince did not arrive
In Land Forgotten's realm
Clad in armor with sword in hand
But dressed like them in rags.

He lived and moved among the slaves
To find his stolen ones.
He sought to show his royal way
To see who would believe:

Believe he was the Great High Prince,
His father's son enthroned;
Believe he came to rescue and
Their birthright to restore;

Believe by faith he'd pay the price
To set them free from hell;
Believe and hope that one day soon
They'd be at home with him.

The Great High Prince these truths did speak,
Proclaimed them boldly left and right.
Both slaves and Satan heard his news:
"I am the way to life."

The slaves rejoiced with hope and joy
To serve the Great High King,
But who could pay the ransom price
To free from Satan's power?

But Satan laughed and mocked and schemed
The Prince's life to take.
The plot was laid, betrayed he'd be
By hand of friend not foe.

The friend did greet him in the night
And so betrayed the Prince.
So off to trial he was led,
False witnesses to hear.

No word he spoke, but like a lamb
To be slain, waited still.
A charge of treason was secured;
The penalty was death.

The Great High Prince to death was led,
Unfolding Satan's plan
To kill the Prince most cruelly,
All evil lay on him.

That day he died both earth and heav'n
The tragedy did mourn;
The earth itself with quaking heaved;
The sun to darkness turned.

His body in a tomb was laid.
The tomb was closed, then sealed;
Satan sent soldiers there to stand
Outside to guard the door.

That grave could not his body keep
For Satan took that life
Against the rule of death which states:
A wrong must have been done.

When in the judgment after death
The records showed no wrong,
No lie, no greed, or angry word,
He innocent was found.

Death could not hold the Great High Prince—
His body surged with life—
His blood was pure and set him free—
He rose to die no more!

The Great High Prince, he paid the price,
The ransom price of blood,
His stolen servants, rescued them,
Their birthright did secure.

The Prince now by his father sits,
His saving work is done.
From here they'll send the Messenger
To lead their stolen home.

And though the vict'ry has been won,
The price paid by the Prince,
Each servant must go forth to ask,
"My Prince, please pay for me."

They cannot go unless they're bid;
The way they do not know.
Unless the Messenger comes forth,
They'll wander aimlessly.

IV. The Messenger and the Child

The Messenger is sent abroad
Like wind upon the waves;
His message touches on the hearts
Of those who stolen were.

He tells the conquest of the Prince,
His act of sacrifice:
He gave his life and lives again,
Their freedom he secured.

By faith the stolen one believes;
The birthright is restored;
His adoption is made final,
Sealed by the Messenger.

The Messenger then trains the child
In ways of royalty:
Its words, its deeds, and perfect truth
That move toward heav'nly realms.

The Messenger prepares the child
To walk the path toward home,
To set his sights upon the heights
And press on toward the goal.

The Messenger goes with the child,
Each step is watched with care
To guarantee the journey's end
Will take him safely home.

And there awaits a welcome true:
The Great High King Himself
With open arms throws wide the doors
And shouts, "My child is home!

"Prepare a feast, my child has come
O'er rugged mountains steep,
Through valleys deep and rivers wide
To claim this seat with me!

"Bring out the robe with train and staff,
My ring place on the hand.
Bedeck the head with crown of gold,
The neck with silver pure.

"Prepare the place for we will dine,
His journey is complete.
He joins the feast with family;
We merry make this day!"

The feasts continue day and night
The welcomes each one sweet;
The father's cheer, "Well done, my child,"
Rests each weary soul.

V. The Call

One day the Great High King says more—
Each soul in awe bows low.
A special message he'll send forth
To daughters far away.

The Messenger will quickly speed
To herald out the news
In Land Forgotten's barrenness,
The grandest call of all.

"Behold, you daughters, hear: My Prince,
No wife, no heir has he;
He seeks a bride to have and hold
Throughout eternity."

The Messenger does take the call
To stolen daughters fair
To see which heart is stirred to go
To be the Prince's bride.

The Messenger along the way
Details rewards for her,
Describes the journey long and hard
Should she accept the call.

She'll put aside her rags of shame,
Her ways of selfishness;
She'll wear the Prince's robe of fame
And walk with royalty.

She'll be arrayed in sparkling jewels,
In lace and satin dress,
On her arms bear bands of gold

Engraved with symbols true:
> A Lamb as slain with glory's hue
> Of vict'ry won o'er death.
> Behind the Lamb a sword displayed
> To show both truth and power.
> Above them both a banner floats:
> "Hallelujah, Amen!"

The journey of that daughter fair
Who seeks the Prince to wed
Demands a cost upon herself
As great as that is gained.

She's called to die to selfishness,
For others give her life.
Her life and breath will only be
All given to the Prince.

Satan and all his evil hosts
Will plague her every step.
Her strong defense is found in him,
The vict'ry of her Prince.

The Messenger will train her well
In art of war and love;
The Prince's word is very truth;
She'll wield it as her sword.

She'll onward march but not alone,
The Messenger is there
To steady every falt'ring step
With promises of truth.

She'll forge the rivers swelling fierce;
She'll plod through snow and rain.
She'll hold his word as life itself,
His promises to claim.

Her cry will wail in pleadings deep
Through suff'ring and distress.
The Messenger will bear her up
On eagle wings to home.

What rapture fills that glorious day
When children all have come!
The family sweet together meet
In joy and love and peace.

VI. The Princess

The Great High King and Great High Prince
With all the family
Have gathered in the dining hall
To wait till she appears.

The Messenger declares aloud
To daughters of the King
These words that stirred their living souls:
"The Princess has not come."

The Messenger each daughter finds
To whisper in her ear,
"Dear child, could you the Princess be?
Your Prince has bid you come."

There alone in a valley cave
A candle all her light,
She felt the breeze and heard its song,
"The Prince does bid you come."

The Messenger now by her side
Speeds her on the way.
The Princess true will heed the call,
She knows he waits for her.

www.ingramcontent.com/pod-product-compliance
Lightning Source LLC
Chambersburg PA
CBHW072038060426
42449CB00010BA/2333